The Commercial Insurance

Buyer's Playbook

How to Buy Smarter Coverage, Avoid Costly Insurance Gaps, and Get Better Results from Your Agent

Samuel J. Summers

The Commercial Insurance Buyer's Playbook

For permission requests, write to the publisher at:

Samuel J. Summers Inc.
Tampa, Florida

The information contained in this book is for general educational purposes only. Please refer to the Disclaimer for full terms of use.

First Edition, 2026

ISBN: 979-8-9962219-9-8

This book is dedicated to God for his grace; to my parents, who always emphasized education and taught me never to stop learning; to my wife Kelly, whose love and support made this possible; to my children Charlie and Riley, who inspire me every single day, my sister Catherine for always keeping my on my ties, and to my mentors along the way. This book wouldn't have been possible without you.

Table of Contents

Disclaimer

This publication is provided for general informational and educational purposes only.

The content of this guide is not intended to constitute legal advice, insurance advice, risk management advice, or a recommendation regarding any specific insurance policy, coverage, carrier, or course of action. Insurance products, policy terms, exclusions, conditions, and availability vary by insurer, jurisdiction, and individual circumstances, and are subject to change.

Readers should not rely on this guide as a substitute for professional advice tailored to their specific situation. All insurance decisions should be evaluated in consultation with qualified insurance professionals, legal counsel, or other appropriate advisors who are familiar with the reader's unique risk profile and regulatory environment.

Examples and illustrations included in this guide are hypothetical and simplified for explanatory purposes. They may not reflect actual policy language or real-world outcomes.

No representation or warranty is made regarding the completeness or accuracy of the information herein, and no liability is assumed for any actions taken or not taken based on the content of this guide.

Introduction

The purpose of this playbook is to provide you, the business owner, with the tools to make more informed insurance decisions. Insurance is often the second highest priced item in a business's overhead, second only to payroll. With such a lofty investment in place, it only makes sense that a little deeper level of knowledge will help your business excel into the entity you dreamed of when forming it.

I know insurance is boring. Everyone thinks so. Well, until you need it at least! Make sure that the coverage you purchase is the coverage you expect to have when a crisis comes. Also, be sure that the agent you hire is capable, that they are there to support you through an occurrence but is also proactively involved in bettering your position in the insurance market.

You will see the term "market" in this guide quite often. "Market" is insurance jargon and is both a noun and a verb. The insurance market is the name for the collective group of insurance carriers writing insurance coverage for your type of entity and in your geographical area. "Taking your business out to market" means submitting your entity to these carriers for coverage consideration, in hopes that you may find improved terms regarding rate, premium, or both.

Terms to Know

Insurance is one of those industries riddled with acronyms. Maybe not to the extent of some industries like the military, but close. It has crossed my mind more than once that when discussing coverage there can be a significant lapse in the point being made when an agent or other insurance professional starts throwing around acronyms, taking for granted that they are being understood fully. This portion of the guide is meant to bridge that gap. The following are terms and acronyms that are fairly commonplace in the insurance industry.

Market, Insurance Market, or Marketplace

These refer to the carriers that could potentially offer insurance coverages for you or your business.

Declarations Page (aka "Dec Page")

A summary of insurance coverage in place or being quoted. These pages include coverage limits, deductibles, carrier ratings, premium, and an overview of coverage forms.

Coverage Forms

The endorsements and exclusions that make up the insurance policy. These explain the extent to which coverage is added or removed. Please review these!

Agent vs. Broker

These terms are a little more interchangeable in the insurance industry. An agent can be viewed as a broker by a client if they are an independent agent representing multiple carriers. Agents can however also utilize a broker (in this case more accurately referred to as a "wholesaler", to access additional carriers beyond those they are directly appointed with. These brokers/wholesalers are typically not directly accessible by an unlicensed individual.

Appointed Agent

An agent that has an agreement in place with a specific carrier which allows the agent to directly represent that carrier.

Appetite

The type of risk that a particular carrier will consider or desires.

COI – Certificate of Insurance

A document that confirms coverage is in place. It states coverage limits, carriers providing the coverage, expiration dates, and basic coverage considerations applicable to the requestor's risk management, including Additional Insured and/or Waiver of Subrogation where applicable.

EOI – Evidence of Insurance

Similar to a COI but pertains to property coverage.

ACORD

Standardized ISO-compliant insurance applications. This is not the word "accord" meaning agreement or a car made by Honda. ACORD is actually an acronym for Association for Cooperative Operations Research and Development, a global non-profit that standardizes these forms.

Supplemental Application

Insurance applications requesting much more detailed information about a company. These have questions targeted toward coverage considerations that provide underwriters with the information they deem necessary to properly underwrite a risk.

Underwriter

An employee of a carrier, brokerage, or MGA who assesses a risk to determine if and at what rate they will offer insurance coverage to a company.

Base Rate

The starting point from which an underwriter will determine pricing for a specific risk.

Credits

Applied by underwriters to decrease rate from the base rate to improve rating based on favorable conditions when assessing a risk.

Debits

Applied by underwriters to increase rate above the base rate based on unfavorable conditions associated with a risk.

Experience Modification (E-MOD or MOD)

A factor that applies to a workers' compensation policy. This calculation factors a company's loss history against its premium paid in, then compares it across other similar entities over a rolling three-year look-back period.

Four-Point

Refers to a "four-point" inspection covering a building's roof, electrical system, plumbing system, and HVAC system.

AI – Additional Insured

An endorsement on a policy that depending on the verbiage, means that your coverage has the ability to apply to benefit another party. These are typical contractual requirements.

WOS – Waiver of Subrogation

An endorsement on a policy that depending on the verbiage, means that your carrier could waive the right to subrogate against another party. This is a fairly common contractual requirement.

PART I

Behind the Scenes of the Insurance Buying Process

Chapter 1 — Why Buying Insurance Still Feels Confusing

Why Experience Doesn't Equal Insight

Most business owners who've been buying commercial insurance for years still feel like they're operating somewhat in the dark. They show up at renewal, review a summary page, approve a premium, and move on. Because nothing catastrophic has happened yet, the process feels like it's working.

Experience buying insurance is not the same as understanding it. You can renew a policy ten times and still not know whether the coverage you're paying for would actually respond the way you expect in a claim. You can compare quotes side by side and not realize that the cheaper option stripped out a coverage form that matters. You can trust your agent for a decade and yet still not know what they're actually paid to do and what they are not.

That gap between experience and insight is what this book is about.

How Complexity Benefits the System, Not the Buyer

Commercial insurance is, by design, a complex product. Policies are dense. Coverage forms are written in legal language. Exclusions are buried. The documents that actually define your coverage, the forms and endorsements themselves, are rarely reviewed by buyers and often not explained by agents.

This complexity isn't accidental. It exists because insurance is a contract, and contracts require precision. But it also means that most buyers are operating at an informational disadvantage. They rely on the very person who is compensated by the transaction; the agent, to tell them whether the transaction is right for them. That's not always a conflict, but it's always a dynamic worth understanding.

The system rewards efficiency, not thoroughness. Agents who write more policies earn more. Carriers that process renewals quickly stay competitive. The incentive structures don't naturally push toward the kind of deep, relationship-driven review that most business owners actually need.

The Illusion of Apples-to-Apples Comparisons

One of the most persistent myths in commercial insurance buying is that comparing quotes is straightforward. You get three quotes, you look at the premiums, and you pick the one that gives you the best value. Simple enough.

Except that it almost never works that way. Two quotes on the same line of coverage can look nearly identical on paper have the same limits, similar premiums, and represent fundamentally different levels of protection. The differences live in the coverage forms: which exclusions apply, how key terms are defined, what endorsements are included or missing, whether the policy is written on an occurrence or claims-made basis.

A buyer who doesn't know to look for those differences will evaluate quotes on price alone. And a buyer who evaluates on price alone will sometimes make the worst possible decision while feeling like they made a smart one.

One of the most important things this guide will give you is the ability to ask better questions of your agent, of your quotes, and of your own coverage assumptions.

Chapter 2 — How Insurance Companies Actually Evaluate Risk

What Underwriters Care About vs. What Buyers Assume

Most buyers think underwriters are primarily interested in what their business does. That's partly true. Your industry classification, your operations, and your revenue are all factors. But underwriters are evaluating risk, not just category. Risk, in their view, is shaped by a lot more than your SIC code.

Underwriters evaluate your loss history, not just whether you've had claims, but how many, of what type, and how they were handled. They look at how your business manages risk internally: do you have safety programs, return-to-work protocols, documented procedures? They look at how you present yourself in the submission. A thorough, clearly organized submission that tells a coherent story about your business signals that you're a serious, manageable risk. A thin, incomplete submission signals the opposite.

Your agent's relationship with the underwriter matters more than most buyers realize. An agent who has a track record of bringing clean, well-documented submissions and whose clients tend to perform well over time gets more attention and often better terms. This is a very important concept.

The insurance industry can be a small world, and reputations travel.

Why Two Companies with Similar Revenue Can Get Radically Different Outcomes

Two businesses in the same industry with similar revenue can receive dramatically different insurance outcomes.

One gets broad coverage at a competitive rate. The other gets restricted terms, a high premium, or declines from multiple carriers.

The reasons are rarely about the businesses themselves. They're about how those businesses are presented to the market. Loss history is the most obvious factor. A business with frequent, small claims is often penalized more than one with a single large but well-explained loss. How losses are characterized matters. How controls are communicated matters. Whether the submission includes a narrative that puts losses in context matters.

This is where having an experienced, engaged agent is worth far more than the commission they earn. A skilled agent doesn't just shop your account, they frame it. They manage how underwriters perceive your business, which shapes the terms you receive.

The Role of Loss Narratives, Controls, and Timing

Gathering loss runs may seem like a cumbersome part of the marketing process, but loss runs are imperative to the underwriting process. If used correctly, they can be a tool to help leverage your business to optimal terms. Loss runs are like a vehicle history report for auto buying, they show loss data over the requested period of time for each line of coverage provided by each applicable carrier. The loss data will show the frequency of losses, severity of losses, and the types of losses that occurred. Most carriers insist on three to five years of loss runs to sufficiently underwrite a risk.

Loss ratios can be used to favorably paint a picture of a business's profitability to a carrier, which can in turn be leveraged for better rates. There are many strategies that can be used for providing loss runs and portraying loss history. It helps to have an agent that will work with you proactively.

Risk management isn't a conversation to be had once a year but is a practice to be implemented continuously. Your goal should always be to hedge against losses, but also to mitigate when they do occur.

Timing also matters. Submitting to the market early; ideally 90 to 120 days before renewal, gives underwriters time to review your account carefully rather than rushing to meet a deadline. Late submissions communicate urgency, and urgency puts you at a disadvantage before the conversation even starts.

Note: The underwriting process takes time. A thorough marketing process takes even more time. Underwriters are generally inundated with submissions and address their submissions accordingly. We all wish turnaround time was quick but that generally isn't possible an underwriter is conducting a thorough review of the risks on their desk.

Chapter 3 — The Insurance Marketplace Is Not Static

Capacity Cycles, Appetites, and Retrenchment

The insurance marketplace is not a static environment. It moves in cycles driven by profitability, catastrophic loss events, investment returns, and regulatory changes. In a "soft" market, carriers compete aggressively for business, premiums are low, and coverage is broad. In a "hard" market, carriers pull back, premiums rise, and some risks become difficult or impossible to place.

Every carrier has an "appetite" which is the types of risk they want to write, in what geographies, at what limits, and under what conditions. Appetite changes. A carrier that actively wrote your industry two years ago may have quietly stopped. A new carrier may have entered the market with aggressive terms. Your agent's job includes knowing who is writing what, and when.

Insurance premiums are determined by underwriters, who assess your business on its merits to determine your rate and thus your premium. A rate is shown on your policy's dec page as well as on quote, and is a factor based on sales, payroll, area, or other pertinent exposures. Note: workers' compensation policies are exclusively based on payroll.

Knowing your actual rate can be a very useful tool, not only for comparing quotes on a more apples-to-apples basis, but also for job costing. Knowing how much you are spending on insurance for every thousand dollars of sales will help with pricing a product or job and will better prepare you for audits.

Why Coverage Disappears Even When Nothing 'Changed'

One of the most disorienting experiences in commercial insurance is finding out that a coverage you've carried for years is suddenly unavailable or is only available at a dramatically higher price, even though your business hasn't changed.

This happens because the market changed. Carriers respond to aggregate loss experience across their entire book of business, not just yours. When property rates increased in Florida as a result of several hurricanes within only a few years and billions of dollars in claims paid out, this was an example of the base rate increasing across the marketplace. In the case of property rates increasing statewide, it is understandable that all properties would take on a rate increase despite whether a singular property had a loss or not.

From the base rate, an underwriter will look at beneficial features of a business or property and items that may not be as advantageous and will apply debits or credits accordingly to arrive at their premium offering. Each carrier has their own unique calculation for determining these rates, which is a contributing factor as to why different carriers produce different premiums for the same risk. These proprietary ratings are a result of that carrier's specific claims experience for the type of risk being considered, how much they are looking to grow their book of business in this space, and other considerations.

How Leverage Shifts Year to Year

Your leverage in the insurance marketplace is not fixed. It shifts based on your loss history, market conditions, carrier appetite, how well you manage the submission process, and yes, you guessed it, your reputation!

Something that can be key to optimizing your coverage results and that is easily overlooked is your reputation in the marketplace. This is an important consideration when marketing a policy. If an underwriter sees your submission every year but never earns your business after they jump through a lot of hoops, your reputation can become that of a non-serious buyer who an underwriter no longer wants to put effort into for maximizing terms. If you are a delinquent bill payer and dodge audits, a carrier may elect not to offer terms to you even if they've never worked with you.

Part of a successful, long-term risk management and really risk finance strategy is maintaining your reputation in the marketplace as a business that insurance carriers want to work with.

PART II

Coverage Nuances Most Buyers Don’t See Until It’s Too Late

Chapter 4 — Where Coverage Gaps Commonly Hide

"Full coverage" doesn't exist!

Sub-Limits, Exclusions, and Definitions

Coverage gaps rarely announce themselves. They hide in the details of a policy that most buyers never read and, in some cases, that agents don't review thoroughly either. The most common hiding places are sub-limits, exclusions, and defined terms.

A sub-limit is a coverage cap within a broader policy limit. Your policy may carry a $2 million general liability limit, but the coverage for a specific type of claim such as products liability, for instance, or damage to rented premises may be capped at $100,000. If that's where your exposure lives, the headline limit is almost meaningless. As you can imagine, a carrier is willing to charge less premium when the bulk of your exposure is relegated.

Exclusions are the provisions that carve out coverage entirely. Every policy has them. The question is whether the exclusions in your policy exclude anything that could actually happen to your business. A policy that excludes water damage from flooding, for example, may feel comprehensive until you're in a flood zone and realize your claim won't be paid.

What keeps you up at night?

Defined terms matter because insurance policies don't use words the way people normally use them. "Occurrence," "property damage," "bodily injury" all of these have specific policy definitions that may be narrower than you expect. A claim that seems obvious gets denied because the triggering event doesn't meet the policy's definition of a covered loss.

Silent Cyber, Contractual Risk, and Professional Liability Gray Zones

Some of the most consequential coverage gaps today exist at the edges of traditional policy categories, areas where coverage is assumed but not confirmed.

Silent cyber is a well-known example. For years, cyber-related losses were neither explicitly covered nor explicitly excluded from general liability and property policies. Carriers have been increasingly adding cyber exclusions to these traditional lines, meaning that businesses relying on their GL or property policy to cover a cyber event may find themselves without coverage. The right place for cyber coverage is a dedicated cyber policy which is something addressed in more depth later in the coverage section of this guide.

Contractual risk is another area where gaps appear. Many business contracts include indemnification language that transfers risk to you. This is language that your insurance may or may not support. If your policy doesn't include a broad form contractual liability endorsement, you may have personally assumed liability that your coverage won't back up. As you can imagine, that could lead to big problems.

Professional liability is a gray zone for more businesses than most buyers realize. If your business provides any form of advice, design, or professional service, even incidentally, you may have professional liability exposure that your general liability policy doesn't cover. Generally speaking, General Liability policies are designed for bodily injury and property damage claims. Errors, omissions, and professional mistakes live in a different policy form entirely.

Why 'We've Always Had This Covered' Is Dangerous

The most dangerous assumption in commercial insurance is continuity. Just because something was covered last year doesn't mean it's covered this year. Policy forms change at renewal. Carriers update exclusions based on their own or industry-wide loss data. Endorsements that were standard on one form may not appear on a renewal with a different carrier.

Business Interruption is a classic example. During COVID there was a massive influx of businesses looking to make Business Interruption claims. Rather BI coverage was in effect or not, the overwhelming response was claim declinations from the carrier. The reason is that BI coverage is (almost) exclusively property coverage. Property claims require there to be property damage to trigger the coverage. There would have to be a triggering cause of loss to property for this coverage to be triggered. In the case of COVID, business was interrupted by an event exclusive of physical damage to covered properties. Businesses that assumed business interruption would "cover something like this" were wrong, not because they were lied to, but because they never fully understood what coverage they purchased.

Always review the forms and let your agent know if there is anything that stands out as a concern. Coverage continuity is worth confirming at every renewal, not assumed.

Chapter 5 — Claims: When Theory Meets Reality

The Difference Between Having Coverage and Successfully Using It

There is a moment in every business owner's life when insurance stops being a line item and becomes a lifeline. That moment is the claim. Claims are where theory meets reality, where the policy you thought you had is tested against the policy you actually bought. The truth is, most buyers don't discover the limitations of their coverage until they're in the middle of a loss, trying to make sense of why something they believed was covered is suddenly being questioned.

It goes something like this: A client calls, shaken and frustrated, because the carrier is hesitating or asking for documentation they don't have, or pointing to an exclusion they didn't know existed. They've been paying premiums faithfully for years. They've never filed a claim. They've always assumed they were protected. And now, in the moment they need their policy the most, they're discovering that assumptions don't hold up in the face of contractual language.

Having coverage and successfully using coverage are two very different things. Coverage on paper is theoretical. It's a promise written into a contract. But successfully using that coverage requires alignment between your operations, your documentation, your contracts, your communication, and the policy language itself. A claim can expose every gap, every assumption, every shortcut, every operational change that wasn't communicated, every missing document, every exclusion that didn't seem important at renewal. A claim is the moment the truth comes out.

Why Coverage Disputes Arise

Coverage disputes rarely appear out of thin air. They generally arise from predictable patterns; misunderstandings, operational changes that were never communicated, missing documentation, or exclusions that contradict what the business actually does. One of the most common reasons a claim goes sideways is painfully simple: the policy excludes the operation involved in the loss. It sounds impossible, but it happens way more often than most would imagine. Businesses evolve. They add services, expand into new territories, take on different types of work, or shift their processes. If those changes aren't communicated to the agent, the policy doesn't evolve with them. Everything looks fine on paper until the day a claim exposes the gap. As in many other aspects of life, communication is key!

Another major source of disputes is the belief that coverage exists because "it was always covered before." That phrase has probably caused more financial damage than any single exclusion ever written. Insurance doesn't operate on precedent. Just because a carrier paid a similar claim five years ago doesn't mean they will pay it today. Policies change. Carriers change. Underwriting guidelines change. Market conditions change. And sometimes, the only thing that hasn't changed is the buyer's assumption that everything is still the same.

Documentation plays a massive role in claims outcomes, and it's one of the most overlooked aspects of risk management. You can have the right coverage and the right carrier, but if you can't produce the contracts, certificates, maintenance logs, safety records, or training documentation the carrier needs, the claim becomes harder to defend. Insurance is built on evidence. If you can't prove what happened or prove that you followed the proper procedures, the carrier is left with gaps they may not be willing to fill.

Contractual risk transfer failures create their own category of disputes. You can have a beautifully structured insurance program, but if your subcontractor agreements are weak, outdated, or missing key language, liability can shift back onto you. I've seen claims where the insured technically had coverage, but because the contract didn't require the other party to carry their own insurance, or didn't include a proper indemnification clause, the carrier ended up defending a loss that should have been transferred. When that happens, the carrier remembers it not just during the claim, but at renewal.

Ambiguous policy language adds another layer of complexity. Insurance policies are insuring agreements, contracts, legal documents, and like any legal document, they can be interpreted in more than one way. The carrier may read a clause one way, the insured another, and suddenly both sides are arguing over the meaning of a single sentence. These disputes aren't always about bad faith or negligence; sometimes they're simply about interpretation. But interpretation can be expensive.

Then there are the claims that trigger multiple policies at once. The ones where General Liability overlaps with Auto, or Professional Liability overlaps with Property, or the Umbrella carrier disagrees with the primary carrier about who should pay first. These situations can turn into a slow-motion tug-of-war, with each carrier pointing to the other. Meanwhile, the insured is stuck in the middle, waiting for someone to take responsibility.

How Claims Handling Decisions Are Influenced Long Before a Loss

What most buyers don't realize is that claims handling is influenced long before a loss ever occurs. Underwriters form impressions of your business based on the quality of your submission, your responsiveness, your safety culture, your loss history, and your documentation practices. A clean, well-organized submission tells a story: this business is responsible, proactive, and serious about risk. A sloppy or incomplete submission tells a different story. Carriers remember which accounts are easy to work with and which ones are not. That memory shows up during claims.

This is why your agent's role during a claim is not optional. A good agent doesn't just forward emails between you and the adjuster. They advocate. They clarify. They help you gather documentation. They push back when something doesn't make sense. They help you understand what is covered and what isn't. They make sure the carrier sees the full context, not just the surface-level facts. A strong agent can mean the difference between a smooth claim and a nightmare.

A well-written narrative, strong risk controls, and clear communication with your agent all contribute to better outcomes when a claim occurs. The difference between a claim that gets resolved efficiently and one that spirals into frustration often comes down to preparation, clarity, and the strength of your agent's involvement. Claims are not just financial events; they are relationship events. They reveal the quality of your insurance program, the accuracy of your communication, and the effectiveness of your agent.

When a claim hits, you don't rise to the level of your expectations, you fall to the level of your preparation. Preparation is built long before the loss ever occurs.

Chapter 6 — The Cost of Over-Insurance and Under-Insurance

Paying for Coverage That Won't Respond

Coinsurance is one of the most impactful and least understood concepts in commercial property insurance, and it is a perfect illustration of how over- or under-insuring a property creates real financial consequences.

I regularly cross paths with seasoned property investors who have been buying properties and property insurance for decades but have never had coinsurance explained. Most property policies have a coinsurance clause. Coinsurance options are generally 100% (least ideal), 90%, or 80% (most ideal of these). An 80% coinsurance clause basically means you have a 20% margin of error between your building limit on your policy and the assessed value of your property by an insurance adjuster at the time of loss. If you are insured below 20% of that assessed value and have an 80% coinsurance clause, your payable limit amount will be reduced as a penalty by the percentage difference you are off.

This is why a 100% coinsurance is least ideal: if you are deemed to be underinsured at all, you are looking at a penalty resulting in a reduced payout.

Replacement costs are generally determined by the Marshall & Swift formula, an industry standard. It calculates the reconstruction cost based on the location, type of construction, occupancy, square footage, and a few other major components. An adjuster will do their best to determine the reconstruction cost at the time of loss, but due to the nature of the situation this is still a subjective result. Because of this, it is advisable to put yourself in the best position proactively or be prepared for the potential of a payout at a fraction of the insured value.

A replacement cost estimate based on the Marshall & Swift formula helps to hedge your bets against the coinsurance clause. An appraisal, however, is best. Having an appraisal every three or so years can also be a good way to be proactive in a claims scenario and is a strong addition to a risk management program.

False Comfort and Uncovered Severity Risk

One of the most dangerous positions a business can find itself in is believing it is well-protected when, in reality, it is exposed in the areas that matter most. This false comfort usually comes from having broad, familiar coverages — the kinds of policies every business buys because they're standard, expected, and easy to understand. A business might carry a solid General Liability policy, a Property policy, maybe even a Workers' Compensation policy with a good experience mod. On paper, it looks like a complete insurance program. The owner feels responsible, diligent, and protected.

But breadth of coverage is not the same as depth of coverage.

Breadth gives you a wide surface area and include many categories of risk addressed at a basic level. Depth protects you where the severity lives; the catastrophic, business-ending scenarios that don't happen often but can destroy everything when they do. A business can have broad coverage and still be one serious claim away from financial collapse. The worst part of this scenario is that most owners don't realize this until after the loss.

I've seen businesses with excellent General Liability coverage but no Professional Liability, even though their operations clearly involve advisory work, design work, or decision-making that could easily trigger a professional exposure. I've seen companies with strong primary policies but no Umbrella or Excess Liability, leaving them exposed to high-severity losses that exceed their limits. I've seen firms with robust property schedules but no Business Income coverage, meaning they could rebuild their building but not survive the months of lost revenue that follow.

This is the danger of feeling "over-insured" simply because you have multiple policies. You can be over-insured on low-severity risks and dramatically under-insured on the ones that actually threaten your survival. A business might have a million dollars of coverage in areas where they'll never have a claim, while carrying only a fraction of what they need in areas where a single incident could cost five million. That imbalance creates a false sense of security or a belief that the insurance program is strong because it looks full, even though it's hollow in the places that matter most.

The truth I've come to realize is that many catastrophic losses don't come from the risks business owners worry about. They come from the risks they assume are already covered. They come from the exclusions they didn't read, the endorsements they didn't understand, the coverage lines they didn't think applied to them, and the limits they didn't realize were inadequate. Catastrophic losses can come from the blind spots, the areas where the business is exposed but unaware.

This is why depth matters. Depth is what protects you from the losses that don't happen often but change everything when they do. Depth is what keeps a lawsuit from wiping out your assets. Depth is what keeps a fire from shutting your doors permanently. Depth is what keeps a professional error from turning into a seven-figure judgment. Depth is what separates businesses that survive from those that don't.

False comfort is the enemy of preparation. And the only way to eliminate false comfort is to understand the difference between feeling insured and actually being insured.

Risk Tolerance vs. Insurance Transfer

Every business has a natural level of risk tolerance, whether they've articulated it or not. Some owners are comfortable taking on more risk because they have strong cash reserves, predictable operations, or a high appetite for volatility. Others prefer to transfer as much risk as possible because they value stability, predictability, and peace of mind. The problem is that most insurance decisions are not made based on risk tolerance. They're made based on budget pressure.

Budget pressure is real but is also the worst possible driver of insurance strategy. It leads to decisions that feel good in the moment but create long-term exposure. It leads to higher deductibles chosen not because the business can absorb the loss, but because the premium difference looked appealing. It leads to declining optional coverages not because the risk is low, but because the cost felt inconvenient. It leads to skipping Umbrella coverage not because the business doesn't need it, but because the owner didn't want to spend another few thousand dollars.

Risk tolerance should drive insurance decisions — not budget pressure.

When a business chooses a deductible, it should be based on what the company can comfortably absorb without disrupting operations. When a business decides whether to purchase an Umbrella policy, it should be based on the severity of the risks they face, not the cost of the premium. When a business evaluates whether to add Professional Liability, Cyber Liability, or Employment Practices Liability, the decision should be based on exposure, not convenience.

This is where captives and dividend-eligible programs come into play. These structures allow businesses to take on more risk intentionally, strategically, and with the potential for financial reward. A captive is not just a funding mechanism; it's a philosophy. It says, "We understand our risks well enough to retain a portion of them, and we want to benefit from our own performance." Dividend programs operate similarly, rewarding businesses that manage their risks effectively with a return of premium. These tools are powerful when used correctly, but they require discipline, documentation, and a clear understanding of the company's true risk tolerance.

The key is intentionality. A business should never stumble into risk retention. It should choose it. It should understand the financial implications, the operational implications, and the long-term impact on the company's stability. Retaining risk can be smart. Transferring risk can be smart. What's dangerous is doing either one without a strategy.

When risk tolerance drives insurance decisions, the program becomes aligned with the company's financial philosophy. When budget pressure drives insurance decisions, the program becomes a patchwork of compromises that only reveal themselves during a claim. And as we've already established, a claim is the worst possible time to discover that your insurance strategy was built on convenience instead of intention.

The businesses that thrive are the ones that understand what risks they can afford to keep and what risks they must transfer. They don't confuse low-severity frequency with high-severity exposure. They don't mistake a full insurance schedule for a complete insurance program. They don't let budget pressure dictate their protection. They build their insurance strategy the same way they build their business, which is deliberately, thoughtfully, and with a clear understanding of what's at stake.

PART III

Brokers, Agents, and the Incentives You Don't See

Chapter 7 — What an Agent Is Paid to Do (and What They Aren't)

Commission Structures and Incentives

The standard compensation model in commercial insurance is commission-based. When an agent or broker places your coverage, they earn a percentage of the premium which is typically somewhere between 10% and 20% depending on the line and carrier, though this varies widely. That commission is paid by the carrier, not invoiced to you directly, which is part of why it's easy to overlook.

This structure creates an inherent dynamic worth understanding: the agent's compensation is tied to the size of your premium. A higher premium means more commission. This doesn't mean that agents are motivated to overcharge you, and most aren't, but it does mean their financial incentive isn't purely aligned with finding you the lowest cost. It's aligned with placing the coverage.

Some agencies also receive contingent commissions or profit-sharing from carriers based on the overall profitability of the business they send. If a carrier's book of business from a particular agency is performing well, meaning claims are low relative to premium, the carrier may pay a bonus to the agency at year's end. This isn't disclosed at the transaction level and rarely surfaces in client conversations.

Why Service Levels Vary

Not every account gets the same level of attention, even within the same agency. Larger accounts with more complex programs tend to receive more dedicated service. Smaller accounts, even if they're significant businesses by any objective measure, may be processed more transactionally.

Service level also varies by the individual agent, not just the agency. An experienced agent with a smaller book may be far more engaged with your account than a high-volume producer at a large firm who treats renewals as processing tasks. The size of the agency is not a proxy for the quality of service your account will receive.

Many agencies pay a lower percentage of commission to their agents which would reduce their incentive to spend as much time on an account after the first renewal.

The Difference Between Access and Advocacy

Beyond shopping for insurance quotes with the hope of finding better rates, it is the role of an agent to identify gaps in coverage or other idiosyncratic issues that can lead to coverage reduction or denial. It is to position you to be viewed in a favorable light for underwriting review. This comes from loss control and risk mitigation practices that an agent and agency should be providing as part of risk management.

Access means the agent can get your submission in front of a carrier. Advocacy means the agent is actively working to frame your risk favorably, explain your losses in context, negotiate terms, and push back when a carrier's offer isn't in your best interest. Most agents provide access. Fewer provide genuine advocacy.

Ultimately, the goal is to position a business well to reduce overhead with competitive rates but also to transfer the risk of the business where able, putting the burden back onto the carrier or other businesses you operate with, such as subcontractors or suppliers.

It is important to find an agent that has access to the best carriers for your business but is also an advocate for your business.

Chapter 8 — Selecting an Agent: Questions Most Buyers Don't Ask

Questions That Reveal Sophistication

Most buyers evaluate agents on two things: how personable they are and how the premium compares to what they're currently paying. Both of those things matter, but neither tells you much about whether the agent is capable of actually serving your account well over time.

Here are the questions worth asking, these are the ones that reveal whether an agent has the knowledge, the relationships, and the orientation to be a real partner:

What carriers are writing businesses like mine, and how many of those carriers do you have access to? How much business do you have with those carriers? This matters because carrier relationships aren't just about access, they're about leverage. An agent who places a significant amount of premium with a given carrier can have a very different conversation than one who submits occasional accounts.

What will you do once the program is put together? What services can I expect? What will you do to help with loss control and to improve my position in the insurance market over time? The answer to this question separates transactional agents from advisory ones. If the answer is essentially "we'll send you renewal reminders and handle certificates," that tells you something.

What role will you play in the event of a loss? Do you have an internal claims team? Any proactive risk management personnel or documentation resources? Claims advocacy is one of the highest-value services an agent can provide and one of the most underdelivered.

Red Flags in Broker Presentations

Watch for proposals that lead with premium reduction above all else. As you've learned, a lower premium is not inherently better. It may reflect stripped coverage forms, higher deductibles, a carrier with a weaker claims reputation, or a move to a non-admitted market without explanation of what that means for you.

Watch for vague answers about coverage differences between the incumbent and the proposed program. An agent who can't tell you specifically what changed deserves more questions. Watch for agents who show up only at renewal and go quiet in between. The relationship between renewal conversations reveals how advisory a relationship actually is.

Perhaps the most common pitfall and one that quietly damages your standing in the market, is allowing multiple agents to compete for your business simultaneously. The diagram below illustrates why this approach consistently produces worse outcomes than working with one well-equipped agent who targets the right carriers from the start.

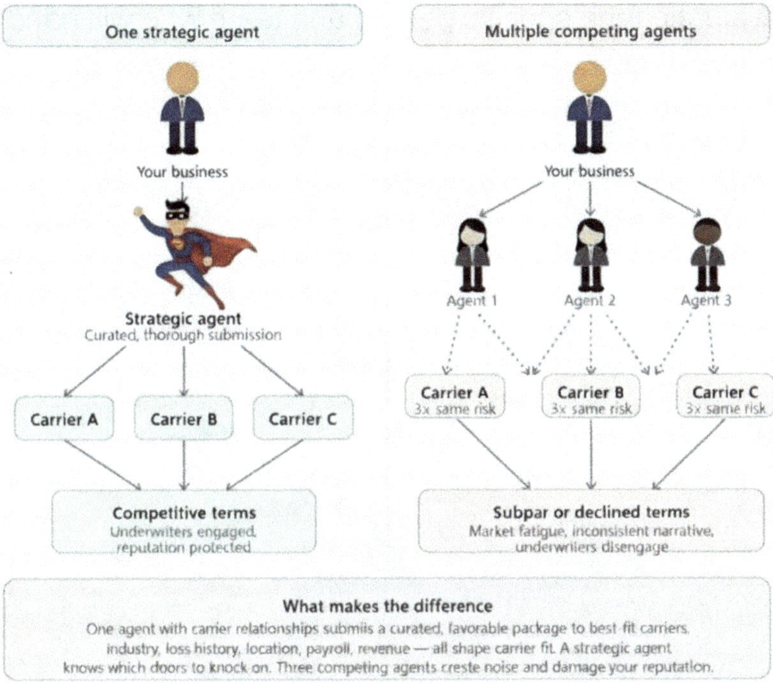

Figure 1: When multiple agents submit the same risk to the same carriers, underwriters receive duplicate submissions with inconsistent narratives. The result is market fatigue, deprioritized accounts, and subpar terms. One strategic agent, with the right carrier relationships and a curated, thorough submission consistently produces better outcomes.

Why Size Alone Is Not a Proxy for Quality

Large national brokerages generally have access to more carriers and may carry more leverage in certain markets. However, the individual who services your account at a large firm may have a much larger book of business, less time per account, and less flexibility than an independent agent or regional firm with a smaller, more focused practice. Size is a factor, but it's not a substitute for evaluating the specific person and team who will handle your account.

Chapter 9 — When an Agent Adds the Most Value — and When They Don't

Transactional vs. Advisory Relationships

There is a fundamental difference between a transactional broker and an advisory relationship, and unfortunately, most business owners don't realize which one they have until something goes wrong. A transactional broker shows up at renewal, gathers the information needed to process the account, sends it to the market, delivers the quote, and disappears until the next renewal cycle. They are polite, responsive when asked, and perfectly capable of placing a policy. But they are not involved in your business. They are not thinking about your risks. They are not anticipating issues before they arise. They are not shaping your position in the market. They are simply executing a transaction.

An advisory relationship looks nothing like that. An advisory agent is present throughout the year, not just at renewal. They initiate conversations about your operations, your contracts, your safety practices, your growth plans, and your exposures. They are a teammate. They bring market intelligence to you and not just pricing trends, but underwriting appetite shifts, carrier behavior patterns, and emerging risks that could affect your business. They help you prepare for renewals months in advance, not days. They work with you on loss control, documentation, and narrative development so that when your account hits an underwriter's desk, it tells the story you want it to tell.

An advisory agent doesn't wait for you to call with a problem. They call you before the problem exists. They help you understand how a change in operations affects your coverage. They help you evaluate whether a contract exposes you to unnecessary liability. They help you build a risk management culture that reduces claims and strengthens your position in the market. They are not just placing insurance; they are shaping your risk strategy.

The difference between transactional and advisory relationships is the difference between reacting and preparing. A transactional agent reacts to what already happened. An advisory agent prepares you for what could happen. In insurance, preparation is everything.

Renewal Execution vs. Risk Strategy

Most business owners believe that the renewal is the strategy. They think the process of gathering information, submitting to carriers, reviewing quotes, and selecting a policy is the core of insurance management. But renewal execution is not a strategy. It is a task. An important one, but still just a task. The strategy is what happens the other eleven months of the year.

Renewal execution is about placing a policy. Risk strategy is about improving your position in the market.

A renewal can be completed in a matter of weeks. A risk strategy is built over time, through consistent communication, proactive planning, and deliberate action. It involves understanding your loss drivers, strengthening your documentation, improving your safety culture, refining your contracts, and presenting your business to the market in a way that reflects your true quality. It involves anticipating underwriting questions before they are asked and addressing concerns before they become obstacles.

An advisory agent guides you through this process. They help you identify the areas where you can improve your risk profile. They help you build a narrative that explains your operations, your controls, and your commitment to safety. They help you prepare for renewals long before the market ever sees your submission. They create touchpoints throughout the year, not just check-ins, but meaningful conversations about your business, your goals, and your exposures. They deliver insights, recommendations, and action steps that strengthen your position.

When renewal season arrives, the work is already done. The submission is clean, complete, and compelling. The underwriter sees a business that is proactive, organized, and serious about risk. The renewal becomes a formality, not a scramble, and the results reflect the preparation.

This is the difference between executing a renewal and building a risk strategy. One is a transaction. The other is a partnership.

Market Fatigue: The Hidden Cost of Shopping Around

The instinct to bring in multiple agents at renewal to create competition and ensure you're getting the best deal certainly is understandable. It feels like exercising due diligence. In practice however, it frequently produces the opposite of what you're after.

When multiple agents submit the same risk to the market simultaneously, carriers receive duplicate submissions with inconsistent narratives. Underwriters, who are managing full workloads and finite time, quickly become aware when a risk is being shopped indiscriminately. The signal it sends is not that you are a serious, desirable account. It signals the opposite. Over time, this damages your reputation in the marketplace and causes underwriters to deprioritize your submission or decline to offer terms altogether. The result is flat pricing at best, and restricted or unavailable coverage at worst.

A good agent already does what you think you're accomplishing by hiring multiple agents. They access multiple carriers, compare terms, and bring you competitive options all through a single, coordinated submission that tells a coherent story about your business. That is the job. If your agent isn't doing that, the answer isn't to add more agents. The answer is to get a better one.

If your current agent lacks the right carrier relationships, isn't proactively managing your risk, or has simply allowed the service to slide, that is a legitimate reason to make a change.

The mechanism for doing so is an Agent of Record Letter, commonly referred to as an AOR. An AOR is a written authorization that transfers the servicing rights on your policy from one agent to another. It is a clean, direct way to move your account without disrupting your coverage or requiring a new application process. When the right agent isn't working your account, executing an AOR and installing one who will, is a far more effective strategy than flooding the market with competing submissions.

The decision of when to stay with your current agent and when to make a change should be driven by honest answers to a few questions: Is your agent proactively engaged throughout the year, or do you only hear from them at renewal? Do they have access to the carriers that are the right fit for your specific risk profile based on your industry, location, loss history, payroll, and revenue? Are they bringing a risk management mindset to the relationship, or simply processing the account? If the answers point to a gap in capability or commitment, that gap compounds over time. The cost of staying with the wrong agent is not always visible in the premium. It often shows up in the claim.

PART IV

Taking Control Without Becoming an Insurance Expert

Chapter 10 — How to Prepare for Renewal Season Strategically

Timing, Data Readiness, and Narrative Control

Most business owners think renewal preparation begins when their agent emails them a list of questions a few weeks before the policy expires. By then, the clock is already working against them. Underwriters are busy, markets are crowded, and the submission is competing with dozens of others that arrived earlier, cleaner, and more complete. Timing matters in insurance more than most people realize. A renewal is not an event, it's a process. The businesses that consistently achieve the best outcomes are the ones that start early, gather the right information, and control their narrative long before the market forms its own opinion.

Renewal preparation should begin months before the expiration date. Not because the paperwork takes that long, but because the story you tell the market takes that long to shape. Underwriters don't just evaluate your operations; they evaluate your trajectory. They want to know whether your risks are increasing or decreasing, whether your controls are strengthening or weakening, whether your claims are being managed effectively, and whether your business is becoming more predictable or more volatile. These are not questions you can answer in a rush.

Data readiness is the foundation of narrative control. Loss runs, updated valuations, payroll projections, revenue estimates, equipment schedules, driver lists, and operational updates all need to be accurate, current, and consistent. When information is incomplete or contradictory, underwriters fill in the gaps themselves and they rarely fill them in your favor. Underwriters respond to ambiguity with increased rates to hedge in their favor or with declining to offer terms. When information is clean, organized, and proactive, the underwriter sees a business that is serious about risk and easy to work with.

Narrative control is the art of telling your story before the market tells it for you. Every business has a story about its operations, its people, its safety culture, its claims, its improvements, and its future. If you don't shape that story intentionally, the underwriter will shape it based on whatever scraps of information they receive. A strong narrative explains not just what you do, but how you do it, why you do it that way, and what you've done to reduce risk. It addresses concerns before they become objections. It highlights strengths before they are overlooked. It frames your business in a way that makes the underwriter want to support you.

This is why timing matters. When you start early, you have the space to gather data, refine your narrative, address issues, and present your business in the best possible light. When you start late, you lose control of the story, and the market fills in the blanks.

What to Fix Six Months Out

Six months before renewal is where the real work begins. This is the window where you can meaningfully influence your underwriting outcome. By the time the submission hits the market, it's too late to fix most of the issues that drive pricing and terms. But six months out, you still have time to strengthen your position.

This is when you document your safety programs. Not just the policies themselves, but the training logs, the meeting notes, toolbox talk minutes, the corrective actions, and the follow-through. Underwriters don't want to see a safety manual that sits on a shelf. They want to see evidence that the manual is alive, used in regular operation, and enforced. This is when you address known hazards, whether it's a piece of equipment that needs repair, a process that needs updating, or a facility improvement that has been delayed. Underwriters notice when risks are ignored, and they reward businesses that take action.

Six months out is also the time to resolve open claims whenever possible. Claims that linger without closure create uncertainty, and uncertainty drives pricing upward. If a claim can be settled, documented, or moved toward resolution, it strengthens your submission. This is also the time to update property valuations. Outdated valuations create problems during claims and raise red flags during underwriting. Accurate valuations show that you understand your exposures and take them seriously.

Loss runs tell a story, and six months out is when you can influence how that story is interpreted. If you've had losses, this is the time to document what you've done to prevent them from happening again. If you've had a clean year, this is the time to highlight the controls that made it possible. Underwriters don't just look at the numbers; they look at the narrative behind the numbers.

The six-month window is where preparation becomes leverage. It's where you turn risk management into underwriting advantage. It's where you shift from being evaluated to being chosen.

How to Improve Outcomes Without Changing Carriers

There is a misconception that the only way to improve pricing or coverage is to shop the market. But not every renewal needs to be shopped. In fact, shopping too frequently can damage your position, create market fatigue, and weaken your long-term relationships with carriers. Many of the best improvements happen within existing carrier relationships and not by switching, but by strengthening.

Carriers reward consistency. They reward businesses that communicate clearly, manage their risks effectively, and provide clean submissions year after year. When you stay with a carrier, you build a history, and develop a track record of performance, responsiveness, and partnership. That history becomes leverage. It allows you to negotiate terms, request enhancements, and advocate for better pricing based on your demonstrated results.

Improved documentation is one of the most powerful levers you have. When you show the carrier that your safety programs are active, your training is consistent, your claims are managed aggressively, and your operations are stable, you give them confidence. Confidence translates into better terms. Loss control initiatives have the same effect. When you implement recommendations, address hazards, and demonstrate a commitment to continuous improvement, the carrier sees you as a lower risk and they will price you accordingly.

Renegotiating terms at renewal is often more effective than going to market. Carriers are more willing to offer concessions to accounts they know and trust than to accounts they've never seen before. They understand your business, your claims history, your controls, and your trajectory. They don't have to guess and when a carrier doesn't have to guess, they can be more competitive.

Improving outcomes without changing carriers is about partnership. It's about showing the carrier that you are invested in the relationship, that you take your risks seriously, and that you are committed to being a better account each year. When you do that, the carrier will generally respond not out of obligation, but out of alignment.

The best insurance outcomes don't come from chasing the market. They come from shaping your place in it.

Chapter 11 — Building an Internal Insurance Decision Framework

Who Should Be Involved (and When)

Insurance decisions are not just insurance decisions, they are operational decisions, financial decisions, legal decisions, and strategic decisions that ripple across the entire organization. Yet in many companies, the responsibility falls on a single person. This is often someone who inherited the task rather than someone who actively sought it out. The result is predictable: decisions are made in isolation, blind spots go unnoticed, and coverage changes are implemented without the people most affected being consulted.

A strong insurance program requires the right internal stakeholders at the table, and it requires them at the right time. Finance, legal, operations, and sometimes HR all have a role to play. Being "involved" doesn't mean sitting through every meeting or reviewing every endorsement. It means understanding how insurance decisions affect their area, providing input when needed, and being notified when changes impact their responsibilities.

Finance should be involved early, because insurance is fundamentally a financial tool, a mechanism for transferring risk in exchange for a predictable cost, ergo "Risk Finance". They need to understand the structure of the program, the deductibles, the retentions, the limits, and the potential volatility. They need to know what exposures the company is keeping and what exposures it is transferring. They need to sign off on decisions that affect cash flow, reserves, and long-term financial stability.

Legal should be involved whenever contracts, indemnification, or compliance are part of the conversation.

They need to know what the insurance covers and what it doesn't, because they are the ones who negotiate the agreements that allocate risk between the company and its partners. They need to be notified of coverage changes that affect contractual obligations. They need to understand the limitations of the policy so they can draft language that protects the company rather than exposing it.

Operations should be involved because they are the ones who live with the risks every day. They know where the exposures are, where the hazards exist, where the processes break down, and where the claims originate. They need to understand how coverage applies to their activities, what documentation is required, and how to report incidents properly. They need to be aware of coverage changes that affect how they work, what they can do, and what they must avoid.

HR may need to be involved when Workers' Compensation, EPLI, benefits-related exposures, or employee-related claims are part of the program. They need to understand reporting requirements, documentation expectations, and the implications of certain coverage decisions.

When these stakeholders are involved at the right time, not after the renewal is complete, but during the planning and evaluation stages the insurance program becomes aligned with the company's actual operations. Decisions become informed rather than reactive; the organization becomes stronger, more coordinated, and more resilient.

The Role of Finance, Legal, and Operations

Each internal function brings a different lens to insurance decisions, and each lens is valuable. Finance looks at insurance through the lens of cost, volatility, and long-term financial impact. They evaluate deductibles, retentions, and the trade-offs between premium savings and retained risk. They understand how a single claim can affect cash flow, reserves, and financial reporting. They see insurance as part of the company's financial architecture, a tool for smoothing volatility and protecting capital.

Legal views insurance through the lens of contracts, indemnification, and liability allocation. They understand how risk is transferred between parties, how contractual obligations interact with policy language, and how coverage limitations can create exposure. They see the gaps that arise when contracts assume coverage that the policy does not provide. They ensure that the company's agreements align with the insurance program rather than contradicting it.

Operations sees insurance through the lens of real-world exposure. They know where the risks actually live, not in theory, but in practice. They understand the processes, the equipment, the people, the hazards, and the near-misses. They know what causes claims and what prevents them. They are the ones who implement safety programs, enforce procedures, and document compliance. In reality, it is their perspective that grounds the insurance program.

When finance, legal, and operations work together, the insurance program becomes more than a set of policies. It becomes a coordinated risk strategy. Finance ensures the program is sustainable. Legal ensures the program is defensible. Operations ensures the program is accurate. It is the agents roll to tie it all together, translating risk into coverage and coverage into protection.

Separating Risk Decisions from Budget Pressure

One of the most important disciplines in commercial insurance is separating risk decisions from budget pressure. Budget pressure is real, and every business feels it. But when budget pressure drives insurance decisions, the results are almost always the same: under-insurance that looks smart in year one and catastrophic in year three.

Budget pressure leads to higher deductibles chosen not because the company can absorb the loss, but because the premium difference looked appealing. It leads to declining optional coverages not because the exposure is low, but because the cost felt inconvenient. It leads to reducing limits not because the risk has changed, but because the renewal increase was uncomfortable. These decisions feel responsible in the moment. They feel efficient. They feel like good financial management...until a claim happens.

Then the decision that saved a few thousand dollars becomes the decision that costs hundreds of thousands or more. Budget-driven insurance decisions are the financial equivalent of skipping maintenance on a machine because the repair bill is annoying. It works until it doesn't, and when it fails, it fails big!

Risk decisions should be made based on exposure, not budget. The company should determine what risks it can afford to retain and what risks it must transfer. It should evaluate the severity of potential losses, the likelihood of those losses, and the financial impact of absorbing them. It should choose deductibles based on cash flow, not convenience. It should choose limits based on exposure, not preference. It should choose coverage based on reality, not optimism.

Budget pressure will always exist. However real risk doesn't care about your budget. Risk doesn't shrink because the renewal increase was uncomfortable. Risk doesn't disappear because the company wanted to save money this year. Risk is what it is and is inherent to your business operations. The companies that survive are the ones that make insurance decisions based on risk and not on the budget line item.

Chapter 12 — What a 'Good' Insurance Program Actually Looks Like

Not the Cheapest

The cheapest insurance program is rarely the best one. This isn't a sales pitch, I promise. It's a structural reality of how coverage works. Lower premiums are achieved through higher deductibles, narrower coverage forms, sub-limits on key exposures, or placement with carriers whose claims handling is slower or more adversarial. All of these trade-offs may be worth making, intentionally, for the right account. But they are trade-offs. A buyer who chases the lowest quote without understanding what they're trading away may feel like they made a smart financial decision right up until a claim is denied.

The coinsurance discussion earlier in this guide is one example. A buyer who insures a $1,000,000 building at $600,000 to save on premium hasn't saved money, instead they've transferred financial risk back to themselves in a way they may not understand until a loss event.

Not the Broadest

On the other end of the spectrum, buying every coverage at the highest available limit isn't the answer either. An insurance program that's broader than your actual risk profile means you're paying for coverage that won't respond to your specific exposures. Coverage decisions should be driven by a realistic assessment of what can actually happen to your business and likelihood of an event occurring, not by a desire to feel maximally protected.

Business Interruption is a useful example. The question isn't whether to buy it, for most businesses it's essential. The question is which extensions of BI coverage are actually relevant to your operation. Dependent property coverage matters if your revenue depends on a key supplier or customer location. Utility interruption coverage matters if a power outage would shut you down. Ingress/egress coverage matters if access to your property is a vulnerability. Extended period of indemnity matters for almost every business that would take time to ramp back up after a major loss. Buying all of them reflexively, or none of them, is less useful than thinking through which ones address your real exposure.

Aligned, Intentional, and Defensible

A good insurance program is one that's aligned with your actual risk profile, built with intention, and structured in a way you can explain and defend. That means you understand why you carry each coverage, what you're protecting against, what you've chosen to retain, and what trade-offs you've made along the way.

It means the coverage forms have been reviewed, not just the dec pages. It means the carrier selection was deliberate with consideration for carrier ratings, claims reputation, and appetite for your type of business. It means your agent has been a real partner in building it, not just a transactional processor.

Risk Management is important for the long and short term. It can keep your costs low in the short term, but savings can be dramatic over the long term. A good risk management program in place can reduce your insurance overhead substantially throughout the life of your business. That's not a promise or idea, it's a reasonable expectation for a buyer who approaches insurance the way this guide describes.

APPENDIX

Coverage Deep Dives

The chapters above focus on how to buy insurance. What follows is a reference section on the major coverage lines, specifically what they are, how they work, and where the nuances are that most buyers don't see until it matters. This section supports the concepts introduced in Parts I–IV and can be referenced as you review your own program.

General Liability

The backbone of your coverage. If "full coverage" were to exist (it doesn't, don't forget that), this would be the modality. It is extremely important to review the coverage forms that can be seen on a policy but also within the declaration pages. These forms make all of the difference in determining what coverage is actually provided.

What Drives the Cost

I get a lot of questions that ultimately come down to what dictates the cost of coverage. I think it is helpful to think of insurance coverage as the buyer placing a bet. The buyer is betting that something will happen to their business; the insurance carrier is betting that there will not be a claim. The premium is effectively the Vegas odds. Underwriters begin by examining the specific classification(s) used to describe your business and the amount of exposure as projected to apply to your business practice. The more hazardous the business and the higher the frequency of that exposure, the higher the premiums. Higher limits requested leads to higher premiums. Reductions in premium come from higher deductibles, exclusions or limitations in the policy form, favorable controls in place from the insured, favorable experience the carrier has had in this space, and favorable loss experience.

Coverages are generally presented in a summary format that looks almost like a table of contents. The form title is presented along with the form number which is either consistent with ISO filings for a standardized format or is a carrier's variation or proprietary form along with the form date. Some carriers don't show the form title at all but will just present a form number. In this case, it is important to understand what forms are being provided.

Always review the forms and let your agent know if there is anything that stands out as a concern.

Claims Made vs. Occurrence

Claims made vs. Occurrence is a very important distinction on any policy coverage form. Having an occurrence basis is preferable, however not always possible. An occurrence-based policy covers a claim that occurs during the policy period that the claim occurred, regardless of when the claim is reported. Alternatively, a claims-made policy only offers coverage during the policy period that a claim both occurred and was reported.

Here is an example of a singular claim and how each policy would respond. Let's assume a policy was written for a grocery store with effective dates of 1/1/2025–1/1/2026. A customer tripped in the store and injured their wrist on 12/30/2025, but the incident wasn't reported until 1/2/2026. If this coverage was written on an occurrence-based policy, the 1/1/2025–1/1/2026 policy would respond since the incident occurred during this policy period. If this coverage was written on a claims-made basis, the 1/1/2025–1/1/2026 policy would not offer coverage because the claim came in after the expiration.

Occurrence-based policies are preferable. I have seen general liability policies written on a claims-made basis to offer trivial savings, but this is not advisable given the vast potential for limiting coverage.

Some forms of coverage such as professional liability, however, are almost exclusively written on a claims-made basis. The reason is that some professional-related claims such as malpractice are discovered several years after they occur. A very important consideration when buying a policy on a claims-made form is the retroactive or "retro" date.

Retro dates should ideally date back to the inception of your professional liability coverage. If a doctor's office opens in 2020 and first purchased professional liability coverage on September 16th of that year, the retro date should reflect September 16th, 2020, on all policy renewals moving forward. This is a mistake that is made from time to time but can lead to a considerable gap in coverage. Also confirm prior acts. Maintaining continuity of the retro date and prior acts works to avoid gaps in coverage.

A final significant consideration for those purchasing claims-made coverage is tail coverage or runoff coverage. Tail coverage or runoff coverage is crucial when making an exit, whether retirement, selling a practice, or otherwise. These coverages extend coverage for trailing years should a prior act surface after there is no longer an active exposure. Tail coverage is meant to extend professional coverage for an additional subsequent three or so years while runoff is generally purchased when an extension of as much as five or six years is needed.

Med Pay and Rented Premises

Med pay is a limit meant to provide coverage for reactive care such as covering an ambulance fee when someone slips and falls in your building. A lesser-known fact is that while these limits are relatively low by design, they don't affect your loss ratio.

The rented premises limit is meant to pay for damage in premises rented to you. The classic example is if you rent an office space, and someone leaves a coffee pot on overnight. The coffee pot catches fire and causes damage within your office space, your rented premises limit would kick in to cover those damages.

Property Insurance

Coinsurance

Hey! Don't look past this part. Coinsurance explained.

I regularly cross paths with seasoned property investors who have been buying properties and property insurance for decades but have never had coinsurance explained to them. Coinsurance can be very impactful during a claim scenario.

Most property policies have a coinsurance clause. Options are generally 100% (least ideal), 90%, or 80% (most ideal). An 80% coinsurance would basically mean you have a 20% margin of error between your building limit on your policy and the assessed value of your property by an insurance adjuster at the time of loss. If you are insured below 20% of that assessed value and have an 80% coinsurance clause, your payable limit amount will be reduced as a penalty by the percentage difference you are off. This is why a 100% coinsurance is least ideal. If you are deemed to be underinsured at all, you face a penalty resulting in a reduced payout.

Here is the coinsurance formula:

$$\text{Claim Payment (before deductible)} = \left(\frac{\text{Amount Carried}}{\text{Amount Required}}\right) \times \text{Loss}$$

Replacement costs are generally determined by the Marshall & Swift formula, an industry standard. It calculates the reconstruction cost based on the location, type of construction, occupancy, square footage, and a few other major components. Because this is still a subjective result, it is advisable to put yourself in the best position proactively. A replacement cost estimate helps hedge against the coinsurance clause. An appraisal, however, is best.

Agreed Value, Replacement Cost, and Actual Cash Value

When looking at a property quote, an important coverage consideration is whether the property limit is being insured to replacement cost, actual cash value, or agreed value.

Agreed value can be ideal if you have a recent appraisal. It is the value that both you, the insured, and the insurance company agree on. This waives the coinsurance clause, making claims much more straightforward. Most insurance companies require the coinsurance clause in their coverage offerings, so agreed value may not always be available, but it is worth asking for.

Replacement cost is the cost to replace the property. Actual cash value is the depreciated cost of the property. To illustrate: imagine you buy a new car for $50,000 and park it in your driveway. A tree falls and crushes it. If covered on a replacement cost basis, you can expect a claim amount equal to the replacement cost of your new vehicle. If covered on an actual cash value basis, an adjuster could deem your vehicle as "used" and suggest a depreciated value. Replacement cost is generally the better coverage option for vehicles, buildings, or other equipment.

Coverage Forms: Basic, Broad, and Special

Property insurance generally has one of three types of coverage forms. This form dictates the breadth of coverage for your property with respect to a covered cause of loss.

The basic coverage form per Insurance Services Office (ISO) includes fire, lightning, explosion, smoke, windstorm, hail, riot, civil commotion, aircraft, vehicles, vandalism, sprinkler leakage, sinkhole collapse, and volcanic action. I would caution that sinkholes, windstorm, and hail are excluded from many basic property coverage options.

The broad coverage form is the next step up, expanding coverage to include falling objects; weight of snow, ice, or sleet; water damage in the form of leakage from appliances; and collapse from specified causes. Again, be sure to read your actual quotes or coverages to look for exclusions.

The special cause of loss form is alternatively referred to as "all risk" coverage. The Special Cause of Loss Form (CP 10 30) includes all perils unless otherwise specified within the policy. The special form is the ideal coverage option when looking for the broadest coverage.

Deductibles: AOP and Wind

There are generally two types of deductibles listed: All Other Perils (AOP) and a wind deductible. The AOP deductible pertains to losses triggered by applicable perils such as fire. The wind deductible is generally listed as a percentage of the total insured value of the structure damaged and not a percentage of the claim value.

While a wind deductible may look small when represented as a percentage, it's important to further explore the impact. A building valued at $1,000,000 with a $1,000 AOP deductible could have a $30,000 wind deductible at 3% for the same building.

Business Interruption

Business interruption (BI) focuses on the financial impact, specifically lost net income and continuing expenses sustained during the period of restoration while repairing physical damage. Generally, the claim must be triggered by physical loss to a scheduled property by a covered cause of loss.

Business Interruption with Extra Expense (BI/EE) adds the benefit of covering additional expenses to avoid or minimize the suspension of business. This helps pay extra to assure you are able to get back in business with minimal downtime.

BI is a part of the property coverage form. During COVID there was a massive influx of businesses looking to make BI claims. Rather than whether BI coverage was in effect or not, the overwhelming response was claim declinations from carriers because BI requires physical damage to a covered property to be triggered. In the case of COVID, business was interrupted by an event exclusive of physical damage to covered properties.

You will note that business interruption is accompanied by a deductible not in dollars but in time, generally 24–72 hours. This is the amount of time a business interruption must continue before coverage kicks in. Higher deductibles lead to lower premiums, but in a loss scenario, hours can be critical.

Business Interruption Extensions

Business Interruption coverage can extend much further than the first-hand direct loss. Depending on the type of business and the factors that drive your revenue, it is worth considering whether any of the following extensions belong in your coverage:

Dependent Properties: If a key vendor shuts down due to a fire, if a major client has a catastrophic loss reducing your revenue, or if a third-party manufacturer critical to your final product is taken offline. Leader properties such as an anchor business like a grocery store in a plaza that drives traffic to your location also fall here.

Utility Services: Interruption caused by power outages, water, communications, or gas.

Service Interruption from Non-Utility Providers: Interruption caused by critical vendors such as payment processors, delivery services, or cloud providers.

Civil Authority: Government action blocks access. Hurricane evacuations, police barricades, or road closures after a building collapse are all examples.

Ingress/Egress: Triggered when you cannot access your property even if it is not damaged. Flooded roads or a bridge collapse are examples.

Communicable Disease: Became much more prevalent as a consideration after COVID. Generally sub-limited when available, and can be triggered by government shutdowns, presence of a virus, or required decontamination.

Cyber: Property policies require physical damage. A BI form may address cyber, but it is important to look to have this included on your cyber policy form specifically.

Supply Chain Disruption: Triggers include trade embargoes, transportation disruptions, or port closures due to labor strikes or congestion. This is actually something of an exception to the physical damage rule.

Ordinance or Law Delays: Can significantly extend the period of interruption if permitting delays or new code requirements slow the rebuild. If you've dealt with permitting, you already understand this exposure.

Extended Period of Indemnity: One of the most overlooked gaps in coverage. With a major cause of loss, it can take time for a business to be fully operational again. Most policies will provide 30 days, but 180–365 days is closer to what most businesses actually need.

Spoilage: Generally triggered by power outages or equipment breakdown. Critical for food-related businesses but also pharmaceutical and other industries reliant on refrigeration.

Interdependency Between Locations: A consideration for businesses with multiple locations. Provides coverage if one facility goes down and impacts the others.

Flood Coverage

Property policies as a rule don't offer flood coverage. Flood coverage applies to waters that rise from below upward. A standard property policy, assuming it is not excluded, would provide coverage for a building that had water intrusion from water coming from above such as a windstorm causing a hole in a roof that allows water to pour in.

Just because your building "isn't in a flood zone" doesn't mean that you should decline coverage. It means that you will get the same limits at an improved premium.

NFIP (National Flood Insurance Program) policies are generally the most comprehensive and cost-effective options. The rate is standardized throughout the varying carriers that offer these. For example, an NFIP policy from The Hartford will be the same cost as one through Nationwide. Binding new flood coverage requires a 30-day waiting period from the time the bind request goes in and the policy is paid in full. If buying a new property, there is an exception, the NFIP will accept your closing date. NFIP caps their building limit at $500,000 for commercial properties, excess flood coverage layers additional limits above that threshold.

Commercial Auto Insurance

Commercial auto insurance is not personal auto insurance. There can be gaps in coverage, and it is important to communicate any changes in drivers, vehicles, or operations as they apply to your commercial auto exposure. Coverage only applies to drivers scheduled on the policy. If a driver takes a vehicle home and a spouse, family member, or friend operates it there could be no coverage.

Covered Auto Symbols

Commercial auto policies use symbols to communicate coverage. Commonly used symbols are 1, 7, 8, and 9.

Symbol 1 = Any Auto: Any auto refers to owned, hired, or non-owned regardless of ownership.

Symbol 7 = Scheduled Autos: Coverage only applies to vehicles scheduled on the policy.

Symbol 8 = Hired Autos: Refers to vehicles rented, leased, or borrowed (not from employees) on behalf of the business. Generally, applies to liability only, not physical damage.

Symbol 9 = Non-Owned Autos: Refers to vehicles owned by employees and used in business for errands, sales calls, jobsite visits, etc.

Symbol 1 offers the broadest coverage but isn't offered by most carriers. Symbol 7 is most common and can be grouped with symbols 8 and 9 to offer similar coverage to Symbol 1. Using Symbol 1 is always preferable as it eliminates potential coverage gaps around newly acquired vehicles, independent contractors, and borrowed vehicles.

Drive Other Car is a coverage that should strongly be considered for executives, owners, and key employees. This endorsement extends coverage should a vehicle ever be used for personal use, especially if these individuals do not have a personal lines auto policy of their own.

If a business does not own any vehicles and thus doesn't carry a commercial auto policy, Hired and Non-Owned Auto (HNOA) coverage can be included on a General Liability policy. This is a crucial coverage and is commonplace.

Business Owners Policy (BOP)

A Business Owners Policy, commonly referred to as a "BOP," is an efficient solution for certain businesses. Generally, smaller, lower-hazard businesses qualify. However, some carriers have been creating BOPs for certain industry segments like artisan contractors that wouldn't have previously been considered for this type of coverage.

General liability is typically the backbone of a BOP, but it also includes coverages pertinent to a business: some cyber, hired and non-owned auto, employment practices liability, business personal property, and even other forms of coverage, all wrapped up into one package. As businesses grow, they typically need more thorough underwriting and benefit from being written independently. The coverages offered by a BOP may have sub-limits and exclusions not suitable for some, but for the right business, a BOP can provide coverages that may not otherwise be accessible due to budgetary constraints.

BOPs are an effective, efficient coverage tool for the right fit. They typically include a fairly extensive list of ancillary coverages and are priced very competitively in many circumstances.

Cyber Liability

Cyber is an interesting one. I hear substantially more cyber-related claims affecting insureds than any other sort of claim these days. Cybercrime is the modern-day Wild West. Cyber criminals don't discriminate when determining target businesses by industry or size. Methods used are vast and prosecution and enforcement is very low.

Cyber events can be a hacker hijacking a computer system and freezing it, inhibiting a business from being able to operate unless a ransom is paid; data mining; or social engineering, which may be the most prevalent.

Social engineering usually starts with a hacker sitting dormant in an email system for around 180 days. They study how the business transacts and communicates. Once they identify a target for instance, a vendor that sends a large invoice, they may manipulate the invoice to include the hacker's banking information instead. Your business pays the invoice. The hacker gets paid. Your vendor doesn't. Your funds are gone.

The breadth of your cyber coverage depends on your risk tolerance. Many carriers will offer a version of cyber coverage but may cover only certain scenarios and may have low or sub-limits. There are also carriers that specialize in cyber coverage and include much more comprehensive coverage options, incident support should a cyber event occur (like negotiators operating on your behalf), and preventative tools to assist with proactive risk management.

It is also worth noting that cyber is a form of coverage I believe is well-placed with a non-admitted carrier. Coverage forms can adapt much more quickly without the filing requirements of admitted carriers, making non-admitted carriers much more agile and better equipped to keep up with the ever-evolving sophistication of cybercrime.

Professional Liability — Errors and Omissions

Professional liability isn't for every business, but in the litigious environment we are in, it is advisable for more businesses than were classically considered. For instance, professional liability is being required by an increasing number of construction companies over the past few years.

When reviewing professional liability insurance coverages, the first thing to note is that these are almost exclusively written on a claims-made basis. Retro dates, tail coverage, and prior acts coverage are all critical considerations that were covered in the General Liability section of this guide.

Beyond a policy's retro date and limits, there should be consideration for defense inside or outside the limits. Defense Inside the Limits (DIL) will only provide policy limits to pay for both defense costs and any award issued by a court ruling or settlement. Defense Outside the Limits (DOL) reserves the policy limits for awards or settlements and pays defense costs additionally. Depending on the industry and claim, legal costs can easily erode a policy limit, leaving an insured without any further limit to pay required awards. The cost difference between DIL and DOL usually isn't prohibitive.

Management Lines

When referencing Management Lines, the key coverage components consist of Directors and Officers, Employment Practices Liability, Fiduciary Liability, and Crime/Fidelity coverages. These coverages are intended to protect officers, board members, or organizations themselves from allegations of mismanagement, negligence, or wrongful employment claims.

Directors & Officers (D&O)

D&O protects leadership members from allegations of mismanagement, poor fiduciary decision-making, or misrepresentation from members, stakeholders, investors, or creditors. Without D&O coverage, individuals serving in leadership could be held personally liable and would be personally responsible for defending themselves. D&O coverage provides protection for those serving in leadership roles, whether on a non-profit board, a community association, or a publicly held corporation.

Employment Practices Liability (EPL)

EPL covers claims including wrongful termination, sexual harassment, discrimination, and other employment-related events. Reflecting on COVID, claims were prevalent from workers stating they were being forced to return to unsafe working conditions. We also see claims from terminated employees alleging wrongful termination or discrimination.

A component of EPL coverage that can be overlooked is Third-Party EPL coverage. This extends EPL to non-employee claims. For example, a hotel guest claiming they were discriminated against by an employee, or an independent contractor claiming sexual harassment from an employee.

Fiduciary Liability

Fiduciary Liability is similar to but broader than Employee Benefit Liability (EBL). It safeguards against mismanagement of employee benefit plans such as a 401k/ERISA. EBL is limited to administrative errors such as failing to enroll an employee in the health benefits plan.

Crime/Fidelity

Crime/Fidelity Insurance protects against dishonesty-related losses including embezzlement, fraud, forgery, and other dishonest acts. Crime coverage could protect a condominium association in a scenario where the property manager is caught skimming funds from the association's operational fund. Having processes involving multiple signatures or third-party bookkeeping are good risk management tools to reduce the risk of these losses. While there can appear to be overlap between crime and cyber policies, it is always important to consider the cause of loss when contemplating coverage, the cause of loss triggering coverage dictates what policy actually responds.

Workers' Compensation

The key to the game here is the term Experience Modification. This is best thought of as your scorecard and is a reflection of your performance over the past three years. When you think about the overhead associated with insurance for a business and couple it with the impact that an experience modification (MOD) can make to that overhead, it is really something to focus on as a pillar of your risk management program. A proactive risk management program can make a big impact and pay dividends...literally!

How MOD Calculations Work

Your MOD serves as a scorecard and your agent should be your coach. MOD calculations look at the costs associated with your losses over a three-year period versus your premium paid in over that same time, which produces a loss ratio. This is then factored against other entities within the same class codes. Because of this you are actually competing against your competitors with regard to workers' compensation, as well as in day-to-day business. Consider it your scorecard.

A MOD of 1.0 is considered neutral. All entities start with a MOD of 1.0 for their first three years in business. A MOD below 1 is a credit MOD; a MOD above 1 is a debit MOD. Your manual workers' compensation premium is factored by your experience modification to produce your actual premium. If your MOD is 0.70, you would be paying 70% of the standard premium. If your experience modification is 1.30, you would be paying 130% of the standard premium. When you consider that insurance is generally the second top-line expense to a business, this is very impactful.

Pick an agent that is equipped AND willing to be your coach.

Standard premium is a product of payroll multiplied by a rate associated with a class code. A roofer is assigned a class code that carries a higher rate than a clerical employee. In the state of Florida, class codes are standardized across all carriers; in most other states these rates vary. In "monopolistic" states, the state provides all workers' compensation.

Dividends and Carrier Selection

What sets a workers' compensation carrier apart, particularly in a state like Florida, is a dividend. Dividends are an opportunity for an insured to earn back a percentage of premium paid throughout the policy period. A dividend can be "flat," meaning losses don't affect the payout, or a sliding dividend, meaning the potential to earn varies based on the insured's loss ratio. Flat dividends are the safer bet; sliding dividends can offer much larger returned-premium potential.

Another consideration when selecting a workers' compensation carrier is the carrier's claims resources. Proactive claims teams can make a huge impact on the claims process, which in turn can make a huge impact on your MOD.

Carrier Ratings

Admitted carriers are backed by state insurance funds. These are safer options with regard to carrier strength and hedging against insolvency. Changing the forms with these carriers takes an extensive approval process, making forms less nimble.

Non-admitted carriers are not state-backed but can be a great tool for coverages such as cyber, where having the ability to adapt forms quickly helps keep up with cyber claims activity.

AM Best is the most trusted rating system and is the standard for carriers with a national footprint. These ratings represent how fiscally stable a carrier is, with A++ being the highest rating. For most industries, an AM Best rating of A- or better is considered acceptable. The rating is generally followed by Roman numerals referencing the Financial Size Category which is a classification of a carrier's reserves. XV is the highest financial reserve classification, equating to more than $2 billion.

A carrier can still be stable but not meet AM Best criteria. For instance, a regional property carrier may be evaluated by Demotech, a trusted evaluator of regional property insurance carriers.

Ratings and FSC are an important consideration in years like 2021 and 2022 in the Florida insurance market, when carriers went into receivership. However, while these ratings and standings are important, they should be a factor for consideration when buying insurance but maybe not the exclusive consideration.

Risk Management

Have you heard the phrase, "the best defense is a strong offense"? Risk management is important for the long and short term. It can keep your costs low in the short term, but savings can be dramatic over the long term. I would argue that having a good risk management program in place can reduce your insurance overhead substantially throughout the life of your business.

Something that can be key to optimizing your coverage results and that is easily overlooked, is your reputation in the marketplace. Both your reputation and your agent's reputation in the marketplace can far precede you. If an underwriter sees your submission every year but never earns your business after jumping through a lot of hoops, your reputation can become that of a non-serious buyer who an underwriter no longer wants to put effort into.

Part of a successful, long-term risk management and risk finance strategy is maintaining your reputation in the marketplace as a business that insurance carriers want to work with.

Return-to-work programs and safety incentives can substantially engage employees, increase commitment to safety, reduce frivolous claims, and propel your risk management program forward. I recommend that my clients send get-well-soon cards and offer safety incentives, for example. These little things can go a long way.

Risk management isn't a conversation to be had once a year, it is a practice to be implemented continuously throughout the year.

Conclusion — Insurance Shouldn't Be a Leap of Faith

We've covered, at a surface level at least, many of the nuances that can significantly impact your commercial insurance buying and risk management experience. Commercial insurance works best when buyers are informed, intentional, and clear about the trade-offs they are making when assessing and buying coverage.

Unfortunately, the structure of the insurance marketplace does not always promote transparency, and over time even experienced buyers can find themselves operating on assumptions rather than insight. The result is often frustration. Not because decisions were made poorly, but because they were made without full visibility into how outcomes are shaped.

This guide was written to provide that visibility.

If it has helped you see your insurance program differently, identify areas worth revisiting, or recognize questions that deserve more thoughtful discussion, then it has accomplished its purpose.

For some organizations, that reflection confirms their current approach.

For others, it highlights opportunities to better align coverage, process, and risk strategy with the realities of the business.

Either outcome is a step toward more intentional decision-making.

Meaningful insurance conversations don't start with products, they start with clarity.

If this guide raised questions about your current approach, those questions are worth exploring…and well before renewal season dictates the conversation.

Glossary

Key terms and acronyms used throughout this book, presented in alphabetical order for quick reference.

A

ACORD Stands for Association for Cooperative Operations Research and Development. A global nonprofit that produces standardized, ISO-compliant insurance application forms used across the industry.

Additional Insured (AI) An endorsement on a policy that extends certain coverage benefits to a third party. The scope of coverage depends on the specific endorsement language. Typically required by contract.

Agent A licensed insurance professional who sells and services insurance policies. May be captive (representing a single carrier) or independent (representing multiple carriers). See also: Broker.

Agent of Record Letter (AOR) A written authorization signed by the policyholder that transfers servicing rights on an existing policy from one agent to another. Does not require a new application or disruption to coverage.

Agreed Value A property valuation method where the insured and insurer agree in advance on the value of the covered property. Waives the coinsurance clause, making claims more straightforward. Requires a current appraisal.

All Other Perils Deductible (AOP) The deductible that applies to most covered property losses, excluding wind and hail (which carry a separate deductible). Expressed as a flat dollar amount.

Appetite The types of risk a carrier actively wants to write. Appetite varies by industry, geography, size, and loss history, and changes over time based on market conditions and the carrier's claims experience.

Appointed Agent An agent who has a formal agreement with a specific carrier to directly represent and place business with that carrier.

Actual Cash Value (ACV) The depreciated value of property at the time of loss. Contrast with Replacement Cost Value, which pays to replace the item without deducting for depreciation.

B

Base Rate The starting point an underwriter uses to price a risk before applying credits or debits based on the specific characteristics of the account.

Broker A licensed intermediary who places insurance on behalf of a client, often accessing multiple carriers. In commercial insurance the terms agent and broker are frequently used interchangeably. Wholesalers are a distinct type of broker not directly accessible to unlicensed individuals.

Business Interruption (BI) A property coverage that reimburses lost net income and continuing expenses during the period of restoration following physical damage to a covered property by a covered cause of loss.

Business Owners Policy (BOP) A bundled insurance package typically available to smaller, lower-hazard businesses. Combines general liability, business personal property, and often several ancillary coverages into a single policy.

C

Certificate of Insurance (COI) A document confirming that insurance coverage is in place. Lists coverage limits, carriers, expiration dates, and any applicable endorsements such as Additional Insured or Waiver of Subrogation.

Claims-Made Policy A policy that covers claims both made and reported during the active policy period.

Common for professional liability. Contrast with Occurrence-Based Policy.

Coinsurance A clause in property policies requiring the insured to carry coverage up to a specified percentage of the property's value. If the insured falls below that threshold, claim payouts are reduced proportionally as a penalty.

Coverage Forms The endorsements and exclusions that define what a policy actually covers. Coverage forms are the substance of the policy and should always be reviewed, not just the declarations page summary.

Credits Reductions applied by an underwriter to the base rate based on favorable characteristics of the risk, such as strong safety programs, favorable loss history, or desirable industry classification.

D

Debits Increases applied by an underwriter to the base rate based on unfavorable characteristics of the risk, such as poor loss history, hazardous operations, or adverse location factors.

Declarations Page (Dec Page) A summary page of a policy listing coverage limits, deductibles, the insuring carrier, premium, and applicable coverage forms. Think of it as the table of contents for your policy… important, but not the whole story.

Defense Inside the Limits (DIL) A policy structure where legal defense costs are paid from within the policy limit, reducing the amount available for settlements or awards. Common in professional liability. Contrast with Defense Outside the Limits.

Defense Outside the Limits (DOL) A policy structure where legal defense costs are paid in addition to the policy limit, preserving the full limit for settlements or awards. Generally, the preferred structure for professional liability.

E

Evidence of Insurance (EOI) Similar to a Certificate of Insurance, but specifically pertaining to property coverage. Commonly required by lenders or property owners.

Experience Modification (E-MOD / MOD) A workers' compensation rating factor calculated from a business's loss history relative to its premium paid, benchmarked against similar businesses over a rolling three-year period. A MOD below 1.0 reduces premium; above 1.0 increases it.

F

Four-Point Inspection A property inspection evaluating four key building systems: roof, electrical, plumbing, and HVAC. Commonly required by carriers before binding or renewing property coverage on older structures.

L

Loss Ratio The ratio of claims paid to premium collected over a given period. A favorable loss ratio signals to carriers that a risk is profitable and well-managed, often resulting in better terms at renewal.

Loss Runs A report from a carrier detailing a business's claim history over a specified period, typically three to five years. Used by underwriters to evaluate a risk and by agents to market an account. Think of them as the CarFax of commercial insurance.

M

Market / Insurance Market / Marketplace The group of carriers that could potentially offer coverage for a given risk. Also used as a verb; to "go to market" means to submit your account to carriers for coverage consideration.

Market Fatigue A condition that occurs when a risk is submitted to too many carriers too frequently, causing underwriters to deprioritize or decline to quote. Often results from multiple agents simultaneously marketing the same account.

N

Non-Admitted Carrier An insurance carrier not licensed by the state and not backed by state guaranty funds. Can offer more flexible coverage forms than admitted carriers, making them well-suited for emerging risks like cyber. Contrast with Admitted Carrier.

NFIP (National Flood Insurance Program) A federally backed program providing flood insurance at standardized rates. Available through multiple carriers at identical pricing. Caps commercial building coverage at $500,000; excess flood coverage provides limits above that threshold.

O

Occurrence-Based Policy A policy that covers claims arising from incidents that occurred during the policy period, regardless of when the claim is reported. Generally preferred over claims-made coverage for general liability.

R

Rate The factor used to calculate premium, expressed per unit of exposure (e.g., per $1,000 of payroll or revenue). Knowing your rate allows for true apples-to-apples comparison between quotes and helps with job costing.

Replacement Cost Value (RCV) The cost to replace damaged property with new property of like kind and quality, without deducting for depreciation. Generally, the preferred valuation method for buildings, vehicles, and equipment.

Retroactive Date (Retro Date) On a claims-made policy, the date from which prior incidents are covered. Should ideally match the inception date of your original coverage. Gaps in the retro date create coverage gaps.

S

Sub-Limit A coverage cap within a broader policy limit that applies to a specific type of claim or peril. A policy with a $2M general liability limit may have a $100,000 sub-limit for a particular exposure. Always check sub-limits against your actual risk.

Supplemental Application A detailed questionnaire used by underwriters to gather information beyond the standard ACORD form. Common for specialty lines or higher-hazard risks. Thorough, accurate responses directly affect the terms offered.

T

Tail Coverage / Runoff Coverage An extension of a claims-made policy purchased when coverage is discontinued, providing protection for incidents that occurred during the policy period but are reported afterward. Critical for professionals retiring, selling a practice, or exiting a business.

U

Underwriter An employee of a carrier, brokerage, or managing general agent (MGA) who evaluates a risk and determines whether and at what rate coverage will be offered. Their assessment is shaped by the quality and completeness of the submission they receive.

W

Waiver of Subrogation (WOS) An endorsement in which the insurer agrees to waive its right to pursue a third party that caused a loss. A common contractual requirement from general contractors, property owners, and other business partners.

Wind Deductible A separate deductible on property policies that applies specifically to wind and hail losses. Typically expressed as a percentage of the total insured value of the structure, not the claim amount and can be significantly larger than the AOP deductible in dollar terms.

About the Author

Samuel J. Summers is a commercial insurance agent and broker with nearly a decade of experience serving clients ranging from small businesses to large commercial enterprises nationwide. He is the founder of Samuel J. Summers Inc. and approaches every client relationship with the same conviction that runs through this book: that informed buyers get better outcomes, and that the right agent makes all the difference.

A fifth-generation Floridian whose family roots trace back to the founding of Jamestown, Sam carries a deep sense of legacy and an equally deep work ethic. He started working at age nine and has never really stopped. That early foundation, shaped by a family with generations of entrepreneurship behind it gave him a firsthand understanding of what it means to build something, protect it, and pass it on.

Sam is a graduate of the University of North Florida. He lives in Florida with his wife Kelly and their children Charlie and Riley.

Work With Me

If this book raised questions about your current insurance program, those questions are worth a real conversation.

Sam works with business owners and organizations nationwide to build commercial insurance programs that are aligned with their actual risk, their growth, and their long-term goals. Whether you are reviewing your existing coverage, preparing for renewal, or starting from scratch, the process begins with clarity. Not a sales pitch.

To book a consultation or strategy call, reach out directly through Samuel J. Summers Inc.

https://www.sjsinsured.com/
https://www.linkedin.com/in/samuel-summers-insurance/

www.ingramcontent.com/pod-product-compliance
Lightning Source LLC
LaVergne TN
LVHW022027051126
851858LV00019B/309/J

* 9 7 9 8 9 9 6 2 2 1 9 9 8 *